EXPLO
W

SOCIAL SCIENCE

Ruth Bader Ginsburg

MICHÈLE DUFRESNE

TABLE OF CONTENTS

The Woman Known as RBG 2

Marriage and Law School 4

Early Career 8

The US Supreme Court 12

The Jabot 14

Her Enduring Legacy 16

Glossary/Index 20

PIONEER VALLEY EDUCATIONAL PRESS, INC

THE WOMAN KNOWN AS RBG

Ruth Bader Ginsburg has spent her life advocating for women's rights and fighting **discrimination**. Some people fondly call her "the **Notorious** RBG," a play on the name of a famous rapper. Ruth is one of nine United States Supreme Court justices and was the second woman ever to be appointed to that position, taking her seat on August 10, 1993.

US Supreme Court, 2017

Ruth was born in New York to Russian Jewish immigrants. As a young girl, she learned to play the cello and enjoyed twirling, tossing her baton at football games. Her friends and family called her Kiki.

Ruth's mother, Celia, was unable to go to college. Instead, Celia worked to help finance her brother's education by working at a garment factory. Ruth's mother died of cancer just before Ruth graduated from high school, so she never got to see the remarkable things her daughter would accomplish. She left Ruth with a strong desire to learn and an understanding of how important it is to care about people and work hard for what you believe in.

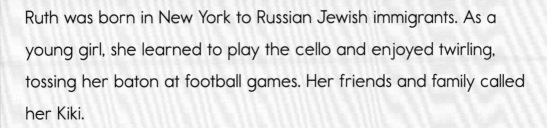

Ruth's mother loved reading and passed that love on to her daughter.

MARRIAGE AND LAW SCHOOL

Ruth studied at Cornell University in upstate New York, where she met her future husband, Martin Ginsburg. She graduated at the top of her class and married Martin soon after.

Ruth and Martin moved to Oklahoma after he was drafted into the military and stationed there. Ruth found a job at a local **Social Security** office. When she told her employer that she was pregnant, her boss said she could no longer travel, and Ruth was **demoted**. At that time, there were no protections for women against this type of discrimination.

MORE TO EXPLORE

When Ruth became pregnant with her **SECOND CHILD,** she did not share the news at work. Instead, she wore baggy clothing and kept her pregnancy a secret.

5

After Martin left the army, he and Ruth both went to Harvard Law School. Ruth was one of only nine women in a class of 500. The head of the law school asked each woman how they justified taking a place in the class that otherwise would have gone to a man. At the time, many people believed a woman's place was in the home, taking care of the household and raising children. Why bother going to law school and taking away a man's career?

Female students faced other **gender** discrimination problems at Harvard. One law library was only for men, so Ruth and other women were not allowed to check out books.

Ruth was the very first female member of the *Harvard Law Review*, an important legal journal.

Gannett House at Harvard Law School

When Martin finished school, he took a law position in New York City. Ruth transferred to Columbia Law School. She tied for first place in her graduating class.

At first, Ruth struggled to get a job as a lawyer because of her gender. Even though she had glowing recommendations and was top in her class, she was rejected by 41 law firms. She was told they did not hire women.

Butler Library at Columbia University

EARLY CAREER

Finally, Ruth was helped by a Columbia professor who recommended her to be a law clerk for a US district judge. Law clerks are usually recent top-performing law school graduates. They assist judges in researching and providing opinions that help them make decisions. Working as a law clerk can lead to more **prestigious** law positions.

Later, Ruth moved with her husband to Sweden, where she translated Swedish law into English. She learned that Sweden had much greater gender equality than the United States.

SWEDEN

UNITED STATES
OF AMERICA

Ruth became fluent in Swedish and cowrote a book on civil procedures in Sweden.

When Ruth and Martin returned from Sweden in 1963, Ruth became a professor at Rutgers Law School and was one of the first 20 women to teach at an American law school. At the time, Ruth was informed that she would be paid less than her male colleagues because she had a husband with a well-paying job. She was told this was only fair since men had families to support and she didn't. She went on to become the first female law professor to earn **tenure** at Columbia Law School.

RUTGERS UNIVERSITY *The State University of New Jersey*

N. J Res 208
Sect 4

SCHOOL OF LAW .
180 Univer.
Newark, New J
Tel. 2c
64

April 15, 1971

The Honorable Emanuel Celler
House of Representatives
Washington, D. C. 20515

Dear Congressman Celler:

I wish to urge your support and cooperation in expediting passage of the Equal Rights Amendment (H.J. Res. 208).

In this critical area of human rights it is regrettable that the United States has delayed assertion of a pace-setting role. Reporting on developments in his country, Sweden's Prime Minister stated during his stay in Washington last year:

"Public opinion is nowadays so well informed that if a politician today should declare that women ought to have a different role than men [in economic and social life] he would be regarded to be of the stone age."

He emphasized that equal rights entailed emancipation of the man as much as the woman. Address by Mr. Olof Palme, the Women's National Democratic Club, Washington, D. C., June 8, 1970.

Although the Women's Equality Act of 1971 is a desirable supplement, it is not a substitute for the statement of basic rights represented by the Equal Rights Amendment.

I very much hope that you will do all that you can to assure that in this nation every person will be given equal opportunity to develop his or her individual talents. Application of this fundamental principle to women is long overdue.

Sincerely,

Ruth Bader Ginsburg
Professor of Law

RBG/em

9

In 1972, Ruth went to work as a lawyer for the American Civil Liberties Union (ACLU). There she began to take on cases that addressed both men and women who had experienced gender discrimination. One case involved a father who was not eligible to receive Social Security benefits after the death of his spouse—a right that women had. She argued to the Supreme Court that the benefits should not be based on someone's gender; instead, they should be equal. She won the case.

“ I try to teach through my opinions, through my speeches, how wrong it is to judge people on the basis of what they look like, color of their skin, whether they're men or women. ”

Ruth took another case that challenged a law that made women's service for jury duty optional. At the time, men were **obligated** to serve on juries, but women could volunteer or refuse altogether. Ruth argued that women's service was just as valuable as men's, and she won.

Altogether, the many cases that Ruth fought and won led to the end of gender discrimination in many parts of the law. The rulings also discouraged organizations from treating men and women differently under the law. Ruth argued six cases on gender discrimination in front of the Supreme Court and won five of them.

THE US SUPREME COURT

In 1980, President Jimmy Carter named Ruth to the US Court of Appeals for the District of Columbia. Then in 1993, she was **nominated** by President Bill Clinton for the US Supreme Court. This is the highest court in the country and makes many important decisions that affect everyone. By a vote of 96 to 3, the Senate voted to confirm her.

Ruth's husband, Martin, stood at her side as she was sworn in as a Supreme Court justice.

In one very important 1996 case, the Supreme Court was asked to decide about letting qualified women into the all-men's Virginia Military Institute (VMI). Ruth and the **majority** of the justices ruled that, yes, women do deserve the same opportunity to attend this college.

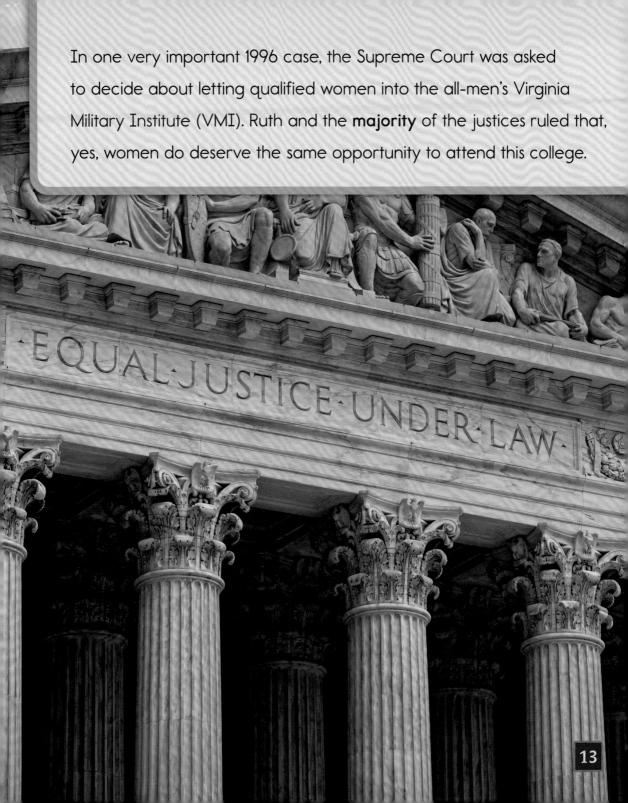

EQUAL·JUSTICE·UNDER·LAW·

THE JABOT

Ruth is well known for the many different collars she wears with her judicial robe. People pay attention to which collar she chooses because they believe it may indicate how Ruth feels about a case.

Supreme Court robes are designed to show a man's shirt collar and tie. So Ruth and another female justice, Sandra Day O'Connor, decided to give their robes a feminine twist by adding collars similar to jabots (*ja-bōs*) worn by European judges.

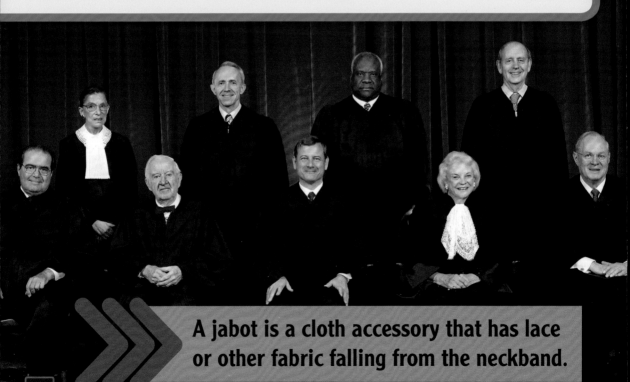

A jabot is a cloth accessory that has lace or other fabric falling from the neckband.

Ruth's famous **dissent** collar has been made into necklaces and pins. Ruth wears this collar when she disagrees with the decision made by the majority of the Supreme Court justices on a particular case.

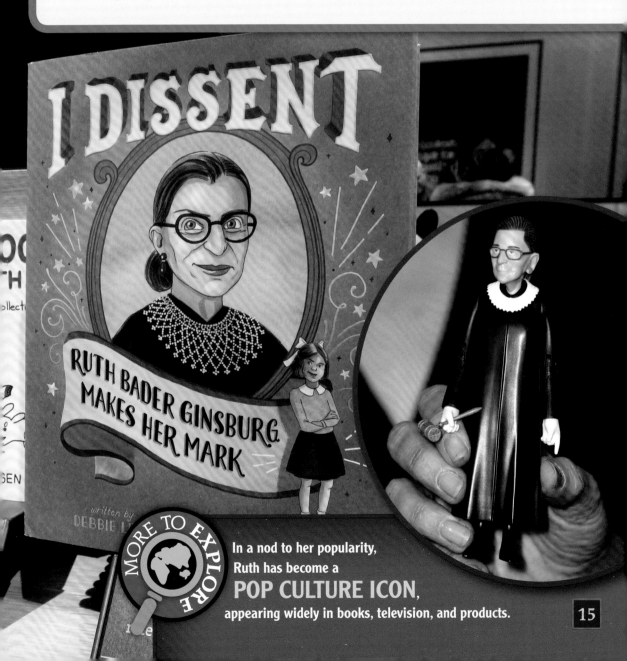

I DISSENT

RUTH BADER GINSBURG MAKES HER MARK

written by
DEBBIE L

MORE TO EXPLORE

In a nod to her popularity, Ruth has become a **POP CULTURE ICON**, appearing widely in books, television, and products.

HER ENDURING LEGACY

Ruth does not believe that judges should make all the important decisions. First as a lawyer and later as a judge, she attacked specific areas of discrimination and violations to women's rights. However, she believes many of these social changes should be advanced by other people, especially the US Congress, which makes many of our laws. Ruth has always advocated for slow and steady changes, feeling that they will be more widely accepted this way.

In more than 25 years on the Supreme Court, Ruth has attended nearly every day of oral arguments, even when she was undergoing chemotherapy for pancreatic cancer or after surgery for colon cancer. She was back at work the day after her husband, Martin, passed away in 2010.

MORE TO EXPLORE

Ruth believes that without the **STRONG SUPPORT** of her husband, she would not have accomplished so much. Martin once said, "I have been supportive of my wife since the beginning of time, and she has been supportive of me. It's not sacrifice; it's family."

Well into her 80s, Ruth Bader Ginsburg continues to make a significant impact on the work of the Supreme Court. Her powerhouse drive extends outside the law as well. She has been working out with a personal trainer for more than two decades, lifting weights and doing push-ups. It's a regimen that helps keep her healthy and strong.

Because there is still work to be done!

MORE TO EXPLORE

While Ruth is known for being a workaholic, she **LOVES THE OPERA**. She even performed in the National Opera once in a speaking role for which she wrote her own lines.

sburg Timeline

1959
Graduated from Columbia Law School

1959–1961
Served as law clerk to Judge Edmund L. Palmieri of the US District Court for the Southern District of NY

1970
Cofounded the *Women's Rights Law Reporter,* the first law journal devoted to gender equality issues

1963–1972
Taught at Rutgers Law School

2002
Inducted into the National Women's Hall of Fame

2010
Received the ABA medal, the American Bar Association's highest honor

Ruth Bader Gin

1933

Born in Brooklyn, NY

1954

Graduated from Cornell University with a BA in government

1980

Nominated by President Carter to the US Court of Appeals for the DC Circuit

1972–1980

Taught at Columbia Law School

1993

Nominated by President Clinton to become the second woman on the US Supreme Court

1996

Wrote the Supreme Court's landmark decision that allowed women to enter the VMI, an elite military college in Virginia

GLOSSARY

demoted
put into a lower-level position

discrimination
the act of treating someone unfairly because of the group they belong to

dissent
a different opinion

gender
being female or male

majority
a number that is greater than half

nominated
chosen for a position, job, or role

notorious
famous

obligated
required

prestigious
admired for its importance

Social Security
a US government program that provides funds for people who cannot work due to age, retirement, or disability

tenure
as a professor, the ability to stay in your job as long as you want

INDEX

American Civil Liberties Union (ACLU) 10
Bill Clinton 12
case 10–11, 13, 14, 15
collar 14–15
Columbia Law School 7, 9
Cornell University 4
Court of Appeals 12
demoted 5

discrimination 2, 5, 6, 10–11, 16
dissent 15
gender 6–7, 8, 10–11
Harvard Law Review 6
Harvard Law School 6
jabot 14
Jimmy Carter 12
judge 8, 14, 16
justice 2, 12, 13, 14, 15
law clerk 8
lawyer 7, 10, 16
majority 13, 15

marriage 4
Martin Ginsburg 4–7, 9, 12, 17
nominated 12
notorious 2
obligated 11
Oklahoma 5
opera 19
pregnant 5
prestigious 8
professor 8, 9, 20
robe 14
Rutgers Law School 9

Sandra Day O'Connor 14
Social Security 5, 10
Supreme Court 2, 10–11, 12–13, 14–15, 17, 18
Sweden 8–9
tenure 9
women's rights 2, 16
working out 18